MINT

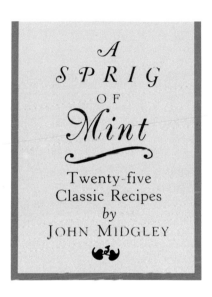

A SPRIG OF Mint

Twenty-five Classic Recipes
by
JOHN MIDGLEY

Illustrated *by*
IAN SIDAWAY

A Bulfinch Press Book
Little, Brown and Company
BOSTON · NEW YORK · TORONTO · LONDON

ACKNOWLEDGEMENTS
The author thanks Sue Midgley and Helen Parker for checking the text,
and Ian Sidaway for his excellent illustrations.

FURTHER READING
The Complete Book of Herbs, by Lesley Bremness (Dorling Kindersley)
The Encyclopedia of Herbs, Spices and Flavourings, by Elisabeth Lambert Ortiz
(Dorling Kindersley)
The Herb Book, by Arabella Boxer and Philippa Black (Octopus)
The Herb Garden, by Sarah Garland (Windward)
History of the English Herb Garden, by Kay Sanecki (Ward Lock)
How to Grow and Use Herbs, by Ann Bonar and Daphne MacCarthy
(Ward Lock)
Wisley Handbooks: Culinary Herbs, by Mary Page and William Stearn
(Cassell for the RHS)

First Edition
ISBN 0-8212-2099-3
A CIP catalogue record for this book is available
from the British Library

Conceived and designed by Andrew Barron and John Midgley

Published simultaneously in the United States of America
by Bulfinch Press, an imprint and trademark of
Little, Brown and Company (Inc.),
in Great Britain by Little, Brown and Company (UK) Ltd.
and in Canada by Little, Brown & Company (Canada) Limited

PRINTED AND BOUND IN ITALY

CONTENTS

ℳINT

Mentha is a large genus, comprising over 600 varieties of mint. Belonging to the *Labiatae* family of plants, mint is related to basil, bergamot, hyssop, lavender, lemon balm, marjoram, rosemary, sage, savory, and thyme. It thrives in many different parts of the world and is a universally popular culinary herb.

Water mint (*Mentha aquatica*) was grown by the Romans and Greeks and is named after the nymph Minthe who, in Greek mythology was turned into a plant by her lover, Pluto. The herb is mentioned in the Bible and wild mint of one kind or another has been gathered since neolithic times.

Spearmint (*Mentha spicata*), the most enduringly popular culinary mint, is native to southern Europe. Otherwise known as 'garden mint', spearmint is a crossbreed of horse mint and round-leaved mint. Also important is black peppermint (*Mentha piperata vulgaris*), a cross between spearmint and water mint, cultivated commercially for its oil, which is used to flavour confectionery and toothpaste. Other popular kinds include: applemint (*Mentha rotundifolia*), a round woolly-leaved variety tasting of apples; pennyroyal (*Mentha pulegium*), a creeping plant with powerfully-scented small leaves that was once very fashionable; round-leaved mint (*Mentha suaveolens*); corn mint (*Mentha arvensis*); white peppermint (*Mentha piperata officinalis*); 'Eau de Cologne' mint (*Mentha piperata citriodora*); horse mint (*Mentha longifolia*); ginger mint (*Mentha gentilis*); Bowles mint (*Mentha rotundifolia 'Bowles'*); Corsican mint (*Mentha requienii*); and pineapple mint (*Mentha suaveolens 'variegata'*). In addition, many of the above have curly variants, denoted by the suffix *crispa*.

Rich in menthol, mint is used in distillation, and as a flavouring in the liqueur *crème de menthe*. It is also used as an aid to digestion, as testified by the many traditional dishes of beans, peas and lentils cooked with mint. Mint tea is also taken as a digestive, especially in North Africa and the Middle East, where a sweetened cup of hot mint tea is the traditional welcoming refreshment offered to guests. Mint is also thought to stimulate the heart and nervous system; menthol is an effective antiseptic, analgesic and decongestant; and mint has even been regarded as an aphrodisiac.

The many varieties and hybrids of mint offer a deliciously varied palate of aromas and flavourings, and are used imaginatively in pot pourris and other aromatic potions.

GROWING MINT

Mint is a very vigorous herbaceous perennial which grows readily in most soils and in any position in the garden. It is always highly invasive and spreads from underground runners. Keeping the plants under control is therefore a greater problem than nurturing them, although some basic rules should be obeyed when growing this herb.

In general, mint will do best when given similar conditions to the damp, shady habitats favoured by wild mint. Moist, fertile soil and a shady or partly shaded position provide the ideal growing environment. The best time for planting is early spring. Pieces of runners with roots attached should be buried at a depth of about 6 cm/$2^1\!/_2$ inches at 15 cm/6 inch intervals. Unless you intend to dedicate an entire bed to mint, it is essential to plant the runners in bottomless containers buried in the soil; otherwise any neighbouring plants will struggle to compete with the rampant herb which tends to exhaust the soil.

Mint is also an ideal container herb requiring very little attention. Potted plants are widely available or simply bury rooted pieces of runners (taken from established plants) in compost in 23 cm/9 inch pots or tubs and water frequently. Whether in the garden or in containers, the plants will need little further attention other than regular watering. Sprigs of mint can be picked as often as required and frequent picking encourages abundant new growth.

The plants will flower in summer and die back in winter. If you want to dry mint, harvest it before the plants start to die back. Hang the bunches in a warm, airy place

(some people put the bunches into paper bags first to catch any falling fragments). When completely dry, discard the twigs and stalks, crumble the leaves between your fingers and store them in air-tight containers.

Many kinds of mint are prone to mint rust, an infection of the fungus *Puccinia menthae* that causes rust-coloured patches to appear on the leaves. Once infection is established, the rust is very hard to eradicate. A common preventive measure is to cover the mint bed with a layer of straw in the winter and burn it. The rust does not penetrate down to the buried runners which are protected from the flames.

COOKING WITH MINT

Mint is an ancient culinary herb that is grown and enjoyed today in many different parts of the world, from south-east Asia, to India, the Middle East, Europe and the Americas. Unlike most other culinary herbs, mint is as appetizing and aromatic in its dried form as it is fresh, and in some cases dried mint is actually preferred. The pretty flowers are also edible and may be used to decorate salads.

The different varieties of mint offer a wide range of aromas and flavours to the experimental cook; but spearmint is definitely the most popular. Mint goes well with all manner of vegetables, especially new potatoes, beans, peas and lentils. Mint also marries very successfully with meats – classically, mint sauce accompanies roast lamb – and is frequently included in dishes of minced (ground) lamb and beef (see pages 32-35, 38). It is superb in salads, especially Lebanese *tabbouleh* which calls for a large quantity of mint and parsley (see page 16). Mint also enhances yoghurt-based dishes such as *cacik* or *tzatziki*, *raita* and cold yoghurt soups (see pages 17, 20 and 22). I also like to flavour pasta sauces with mint and discovered while preparing recipes for this book that it makes superb *pesto* (for which recipes appear on pages 28 and 30). Mint and basil complement each other deliciously, a sublime partnership that is often celebrated in Thai cooking.

With its sweet taste and aroma, mint is an ideal herb to flavour hot and cold drinks, makes a wonderful tea, and adds a special quality to sweet fruit desserts, jams, jellies and preserves. Like other aromatic herbs, mint also makes good cold sauces and condiments such as flavoured butters, oils and vinegars.

Mint is usually finely chopped and added towards the end of the cooking, but it is also robust enough to withstand longer cooking without loss of flavour and aroma.

When buying fresh mint, avoid bunches with limp or yellowing leaves. Fresh mint can be stored for up to three days in the refrigerator, wrapped in plastic while dried mint keeps well in an air-tight container.

The following recipes are mostly traditional dishes culled from different countries such as Thailand, India, Greece and Turkey, with a few of my own creations added to the pot for good measure.

MINT JULEPS

You will need plenty of crushed ice to make this famous Kentucky drink: the contents of several ice-cube trays, briefly crushed in a food processor should provide enough. Serve on a balmy summer evening for maximum enjoyment. Makes 4 juleps.

4 tsp sugar
12 ice cubes
a little water
12 sprigs of mint
enough crushed ice to fill 4 tall glasses
140 ml/5 fl oz/¼ cup bourbon

Frost 4 tall glasses by leaving them in the freezer for a short time. Put the sugar, the ice cubes and a splash of water into a jug. Stir around, allowing the ice to melt a little and the sugar to dissolve. Add half of the mint to the jug. Fill the jug with the crushed ice and the bourbon. Stir around, then divide the contents of the jug equally between the 4 frosted glasses. Decorate with the remaining sprigs of mint and serve the juleps with straws while still very cold.

MINT LASSI

This cooling yoghurt drink from India can be made either sweet or salty, and the dried mint gives it a delicious flavour. This recipe makes 4 large glasses of *lassi*. Drink *lassi* on its own as a refreshing non-alcoholic drink, or serve it with spicy food, especially Indian dishes.

170 ml/6 fl oz/³/₄ cup strained live yoghurt
560 ml/1 pint/2 cups cold water
12-16 ice cubes
1 tsp salt or 4 tsp sugar
¹/₂ tsp ground cumin
1-2 tsp dried mint

Scoop out the yoghurt into a jug, and whisk, adding the water little by little. Keep whisking until the liquid is frothy. Stir in the ice cubes, salt or sugar, cumin and mint and serve straight away or keep refrigerated for a few hours.

$\mathcal{M}$ INT TEA

Mint tea is especially popular in Morocco where it is taken very sweet. Dried mint is preferable to fresh. Makes a small pot of tea.

1-2 tbs dried mint
225 ml/8 fl oz/1 cup boiling water
a pot of freshly-made China tea
¹/₂ a lemon, thinly sliced
sugar or clear honey

Steep the mint in the boiling water for about 3 minutes. While it steeps make a small pot of China tea and allow to infuse. Strain the mint water and pour it into the tea pot. Stir once, serve immediately with the lemon slices and sweeten to taste with sugar or honey.

MINT BUTTER

Pats of mint butter are excellent added to piping hot boiled new potatoes. Mint butter is also very good piled over split baked potatoes, stirred into a steaming dish of boiled fresh garden peas, or served with other cooked vegetables such as carrots and green beans.

110 g/4 oz butter, at room temperature
small clove of garlic, peeled and finely chopped
handful of fresh mint, washed and very finely chopped
1 tbs lemon juice
salt and freshly milled black pepper

Mash the butter with a fork until soft. Mix in the remaining ingredients and mash thoroughly. Shape the mixture into a roll, wrap in foil and refrigerate. Cut off pats of mint butter as required. The butter will keep for about 1 week.

TRADITIONAL MINT SAUCE

There are few dishes more quintessentially British than roast lamb with mint sauce. Here is a traditional, very authentic recipe for the sauce which uses plenty of fresh mint leaves. Roast the lamb to your personal taste and serve with the sauce, roast potatoes and some steamed, buttered vegetables.

small bunch of fresh mint, washed and very finely chopped
1 tsp sugar
pinch of salt
3 tbs wine vinegar
3 tbs boiling water

Put the mint into a small bowl. Dissolve the sugar and salt in the vinegar. Pour the water over the mint, stir in the vinegar mixture and allow to cool. Do not keep for more than 2 hours.

MINT VINEGAR

Mint vinegar may be used to dress salads and is a delicious ingredient in marinades. Fresh young leaves are preferable to older ones and quite a large quantity is required.

fresh mint leaves to fill a teacup, loosely packed
350 ml/12 fl oz/1½ cups white wine or cider vinegar

Wash the mint, discarding any stalks. Pat dry and stuff the leaves into a clean 350 ml/12 fl oz bottle with a screw-on cap or stopper.

Heat the vinegar without boiling it. Pour it into the bottle to cover the mint. Allow to cool before sealing. Leave to infuse for 1-2 weeks, strain into a fresh, clean bottle and decorate with a fresh sprig of mint.

$\mathscr{P}$OTATO SALAD WITH MINT AND CHIVES

Too often, potato salads are drowned in mayonnaise, usually of inferior quality, which can mask the flavour of really good new potatoes. This lighter version is excellent. Any firm, waxy salad potato varieties work equally well – try Pink Fir Apple, Belle de Fontanay, Jersey Royal or La Ratte. Serves 4 people.

675 g/1½ lb salad potatoes, well washed but unpeeled
6 sprigs of mint
4 tbs olive oil
1 tbs sherry vinegar
1 tsp mustard
salt and freshly milled black pepper
110 ml/4 fl oz/½ cup sour cream or
double cream with a few drops of lemon juice
small bunch of fresh chives, washed and finely chopped
4 spring onions (scallions), washed and finely chopped

Steam or boil the potatoes with 3 sprigs of mint until tender; do not overcook them. Meanwhile, chop the remaining mint and set it aside.

Beat the olive oil with the vinegar, mustard and seasoning. Drain the potatoes well and cut them into chunks unless they are very small. Put them into a bowl. Beat the dressing again and pour it over the potatoes while they are still hot, turning a few times. When they have cooled, fold in the sour cream (double cream can be soured with a few drops of lemon juice, beaten with a fork to stiffen it). Add the chives, the chopped mint and the spring onions, season lightly and mix thoroughly. Serve immediately or refrigerate until required.

$\mathcal{T}$ABBOULEH

This Lebanese salad has become very popular throughout the Middle East. It is made with *bulgur* (partly-cooked, fine cracked wheat), plenty of finely chopped fresh mint and parsley, olive oil and lemon juice. This version makes a good *meze* or appetizer for 4 people.

225 g/8 oz bulgur
900 ml/2 pints/4 cups water
juice of 1 lemon
225 ml/8 fl oz/1 cup olive oil
bunch of flat-leaf parsley, washed and finely chopped
bunch of mint leaves, washed and finely chopped
225 g/8 oz ripe tomatoes, finely diced
1 'little gem' lettuce or the heart of a Cos (romaine) lettuce,
finely shredded
4 spring onions (scallions), washed and thinly sliced
1 clove of garlic, peeled and finely chopped
salt and freshly milled black pepper

Bring half of the water to the boil and simmer the *bulgur* for 10 minutes. (The water will all be absorbed.)

Cover with the remaining water and soak for 10 more minutes. Drain very thoroughly. Combine with all the remaining ingredients, season well and mix again. Leave for 30 minutes to 1 hour to allow the flavours to develop and serve with *pitta* bread.

CACIK

This delicious Turkish *meze* or appetizer is also very popular in Greece where it is known as *tzatziki*. Serve with raw vegetables, *pitta* bread and some luscious olives. It is best to use small Mediterranean cucumbers but ordinary cucumbers are fine. This makes enough for 4 people.

1 medium, or 2 small cucumbers, washed and peeled
225 ml/8 fl oz/1 cup strained yoghurt
½ tsp salt
1 clove of garlic, peeled and very finely chopped
leaves from 2-3 sprigs of fresh mint, very finely chopped

Cut the cucumber in half from end to end. Scoop out and discard the seedy central strip. Grate the flesh coarsely, then squeeze out as much water as possible with your hands. Set aside in a colander to drain further.

In a bowl, beat the yoghurt with the salt until creamy, then mix in the grated cucumber, garlic and mint. Cover, refrigerate and serve chilled. Mix thoroughly before serving.

17

$\mathscr{S}$PLIT-PEA SOUP WITH PARMA HAM AND MINT

Here is a recipe to bring comfort in cold weather, and which uses dried mint. This traditional soup is highly flavoured and very satisfying. It makes plenty for 6 people.

225 g/8 oz green or yellow split peas
2 medium-sized, floury potatoes, peeled and diced
water
salt
4 tbs olive oil
50 g/2 oz Parma *ham, cut into small pieces*
1 medium onion, finely chopped
1 clove of garlic, peeled and chopped
1¼ litres/2½ pints/5 cups chicken stock (broth)
2 tsp dried mint
salt and freshly milled black pepper

Put the peas and the potatoes into a pot, pour in enough salted water to give a 4 cm/1¾ inch covering and bring to the boil. Removing the scum, simmer until the potatoes are soft and the water has evaporated or been absorbed.

Heat the olive oil in a fresh soup pot and fry the ham, onion and garlic over a high heat for about 2 minutes. Reduce the heat and sauté for 1 minute longer. Add the split peas and the potatoes, the stock, and the dried mint. Bring to the boil, then reduce the heat and simmer with the lid just ajar for 1 hour, stirring occasionally. Season well and continue to simmer for 15 minutes longer, stirring a few times. By now, the peas and potatoes should have dissolved to thicken the soup. Serve very hot with sliced crusty bread or croûtons.

YOGHURT AND MINT SOUP

Cold soups based on yoghurt, crushed nuts and mint are popular from the Caucasus down to northern India. This delicious version is especially refreshing on a hot summer's day and makes enough to serve 4 people.

280 ml/10 fl oz/1¼ cups strained yoghurt
450 ml/16 fl oz/2 cups cold vegetable stock
23 cm/9 inch piece of cucumber, peeled and very finely chopped
salt and freshly milled black pepper
1 clove of garlic, peeled
50 g/2 oz blanched almonds or pine nuts
2 tbs olive oil
½ tsp cumin, ground
handful of fresh mint, washed and finely chopped
a few ice cubes
sprigs of mint, to garnish

In a very large bowl, beat the yoghurt with a fork until creamy. Stir in the stock and cucumber and season with salt and freshly milled black pepper.

In a mortar or food processor, pound or process the garlic, almonds, olive oil, cumin and mint to a paste. Mix thoroughly into the soup, float some ice cubes in it and serve, garnished with sprigs of mint.

GLAZED ROOT VEGETABLES

These root vegetables are boiled until just tender, then glazed in a residue of butter and sugar and garnished with plenty of fresh mint and parsley. Serve as a vegetable accompaniment to roasts and stews. For 6 people.

450 g/1 lb carrots, trimmed and scrubbed
225 g/8 oz piece of celeriac (celery root), peeled
225 g/8 oz small, young turnips, peeled
water, to just cover the vegetables
110 g/4 oz butter
1 tsp salt
1 tsp sugar
leaves from 4 sprigs of fresh mint, washed and chopped
small handful of fresh parsley, washed and chopped
freshly milled black pepper

Chop the carrots into even segments, each about 1 cm/½ inch thick. (Small baby carrots can be left whole.) Cut the celeriac and turnips into similar-sized chunks. Transfer them to a pot and just cover them with fresh water. Add the butter, salt and sugar and bring to the boil. Cook, uncovered, until the water has boiled away. Stirring frequently, glaze the vegetables in the buttery residue, until lightly coloured. Add the herbs and black pepper, mix well, and serve.

$\mathcal{M}$INT RAITA

Raita is a spicier Indian version of the traditional cucumber and yoghurt salads that are very popular in Greece and Turkey. While the latter are normally served with bread as an appetizing dip, *raita* is more suitable as an accompaniment to Indian meat and poultry dishes.

170 ml/6 fl oz/³/₄ cup strained live yoghurt
225 g/8 oz cucumber, peeled and very finely chopped
1 green chili pepper, seeded and finely chopped
1 tsp salt
1 tsp ground cumin
1 tsp ground coriander
handful of fresh mint, washed and finely chopped

Beat the yoghurt with a fork until creamy. Mix in the remaining ingredients and serve straight away, or cover and refrigerate until required (mix thoroughly before serving).

$\mathscr{M}$ACARONIA

Not all pasta is Italian. Whether pasta was a Chinese invention, brought back to Italy by Marco Polo, or whether the ancient Greeks discovered it first and introduced it to their southern Italian colony of Magna Graeca is hotly debated. Whichever theory is true, modern Greeks are very fond of pasta and serve it in a variety of ways. (*Macaronia* is actually their generic word for pasta.) This dish is much nicer than any bland travesty made with a ready-made sauce. Accompanied by a salad, it serves 4 people.

400 g/14 oz macaroni
110 g/4 oz halloumi *or cheddar cheese, grated*
60 g/3 oz butter, at room temperature
freshly milled black pepper
¹/₂ tsp dried mint

Bring a large pot of salted water to a rapid boil. Immerse the macaroni and boil until tender. Drain well and mix in the cheese, butter, freshly milled black pepper and the mint. Combine very thoroughly and serve.

$\mathcal{R}$ISOTTO OF FRESH PLUM TOMATOES AND MINT

A fine example of summer cooking, this excellent vegetarian risotto should only be attempted in season, when the ingredients are cheap, plentiful and in their prime. Served with crusty bread, this recipe makes an elegant, tasty starter for 6 or a light lunch for 4 people.

675 g/1½ lb ripe, very red plum tomatoes
60 g/3 oz butter
1 tbs olive oil
1 medium onion, peeled and finely chopped
2 cloves of garlic, peeled and chopped
1 tsp 'triple concentrated' tomato paste or
3 tsp ordinary tomato purée (paste)
salt and freshly milled black pepper
275 g/10 oz/1½ cups arborio rice
1¼ litres/2½ pints/5 cups hot vegetable stock
75 g/3 oz freshly grated parmesan cheese
handful of fresh mint, washed and chopped

Bring a pot of water to the boil. Immerse the tomatoes for 30 seconds, remove and drain them. Slip off the skins and dice the flesh.

Heat two-thirds of the butter and the oil in a wide, heavy frying pan (preferably a very well-seasoned or non-stick one). Sauté the onion and garlic until soft. Add the tomatoes and the tomato purée, season and cook over a medium heat for about 5 minutes, stirring frequently. Add the rice and mix thoroughly so that all the grains are well coated with the tomato sauce. Add a little hot stock and stir until the liquid has mostly evaporated. Continue to add the stock in this way, stirring all the while and scraping the bottom of the pan from time to time to loosen any rice that sticks to the base. The rice should be tender and the stock used up after 25-30 minutes. Remove from the heat, stir in the remaining butter, half of the cheese, and all of the mint. Allow the risotto to rest for a few minutes and serve with the remaining cheese.

$\mathscr{S}$PAGHETTI WITH PATTI-PAN SQUASH

Patti-pan squash are tiny, delicious early summer squashes that are picked while young and firm. They make a delicious pasta sauce, but baby courgettes (zucchini) are an excellent substitute.

400 g/14 oz spaghetti or bucatini
225 g/8 oz patti-pan *squash* or *baby courgettes, washed*
4 tbs olive oil
1 small onion, peeled and chopped
1 clove of garlic, peeled and chopped
1 sweet red pepper, diced
140 ml/5 fl oz/²⁄₃ cup crushed tomatoes
salt and freshly milled black pepper
3 sprigs each of mint and basil, washed and chopped
75 g/3 oz freshly grated parmesan cheese

Bring a very large pot of salted water to a rolling boil and cook the pasta until *al dente.* Meanwhile make the sauce.

Top and tail the squash or courgettes. Cut them into fingernail-size dice. Heat the olive oil in a pan. Add the onion and garlic and fry briefly. Add the squash or courgettes and the diced pepper. Sauté for 5 minutes, add the tomatoes and season. Cover the pan and simmer for 5 more minutes. Drain the pasta as soon as it is tender. Combine with the sauce, herbs and half of the cheese. Serve immediately. The remaining cheese can be served in a separate bowl.

$\mathscr{M}$INT AND PISTACHIO PESTO

Fresh mint, parsley and basil combined with pistachio nuts make a most intriguing and delicious *pesto*. Serve with any long type of pasta, such as *linguine, bucatini, spaghetti alla chitarra* or *spaghettini*. Makes enough for 4 people.

handful of mint, washed
handful of flat-leaved parsley, washed
6 sprigs of basil, washed
1 clove of garlic, peeled
50 g/2 oz pistachio nuts, shelled
225 ml/8 fl oz/1 cup extra virgin olive oil
salt and freshly milled black pepper
75 g/3 oz parmesan, freshly grated
400 g/14 oz long pasta

In a food processor, grind the herbs, garlic, and pistachio nuts to a paste, slowly adding the oil. Season the *pesto* and mix in half of the parmesan cheese.

Meanwhile, bring a large pot of salted water to the boil. Add the pasta and cook until *al dente*. Drain and mix thoroughly with the *pesto*. Serve the remaining parmesan in a separate bowl.

$\mathscr{F}$ARFALLE WITH FRESH PEAS AND MINT

This southern Italian dish is a wonderful blend of flavours and textures and is all the better for being exceptionally easy and quick to prepare. If you cannot find *farfalle* (pasta bows) substitute *fusilli* (spirals) or any other stubby pasta shapes. Serve accompanied by crusty bread. This makes enough for 4 people.

1 medium onion, peeled
110 ml/4 fl oz/½ cup extra virgin olive oil
4 slices of pancetta *or* bacon, *finely diced*
1 clove of garlic, peeled and chopped
1 dried chili pepper, crumbled
450 g/1 lb fresh peas (shelled weight), washed
handful of fresh mint, washed and chopped
salt and freshly milled black pepper
400 g/14 oz pasta
110 g/4 oz freshly grated parmesan cheese

Slice the onion in half from end to end. Slice each hemisphere thinly. Heat the olive oil and fry the bacon briefly. Before it turns crisp, add the onion, garlic and chili. Throw in the peas and mint, and season. Cook very gently for 10-12 minutes while you boil the pasta in a very large pot of fast-boiling water. Drain the pasta when it is *al dente* and mix thoroughly with the peas. Sprinkle with half of the parmesan and serve immediately. The remaining cheese can be served in a separate bowl.

CHICKEN BREASTS WITH LIME, MINT PESTO AND HONEY

A long marinating in lime tenderizes these delicious chicken breasts which are subsequently cooked in honey and wine, and then enriched with a mint and pistachio *pesto*. Sautéd potatoes and an elegant salad of mixed exotic leaves make very good accompaniments. Serves 4 people.

4 corn-fed or free-range chicken breasts, skins left on
grated peel and juice of 4 washed limes
2 cloves of garlic, peeled
pinch of salt
generous handful of mint leaves, washed
4 tbs extra virgin olive oil
75 g/3 oz shelled pistachio nuts
2 tbs olive oil
25 g/1 oz butter
4 tbs clear honey
6 tbs white wine
salt and freshly milled black pepper
4 sprigs of mint

Put the chicken breasts into a wide bowl and prick them all over with a fork. Spread the lime peel and juice over them, turn them a few times to coat thoroughly and cover the bowl. Refrigerate for 24-48 hours.

Pound the garlic with the salt, mint leaves, the extra virgin olive oil and pistachios. Put aside.

Remove the chicken breasts from the marinade. Heat the olive oil and the butter in a heavy pan with a lid. Before the butter burns, add the chicken breasts. Fry them over a moderate heat until both sides are golden. Pour the honey and wine over the chicken breasts, season and cover. Reduce the heat to very low and simmer for 15 minutes, turning and basting the breasts a few times. Spread the mint *pesto* over the chicken breasts, cover and heat gently for 3 minutes. Serve the chicken breasts on warmed plates, garnished with the sprigs of mint.

OFTAS

These spicy Turkish kebabs really deserve to be barbecued but can also be grilled (broiled) conventionally, although they will lack that delicious smokey char-grilled flavour. The Greeks make similar meatballs which they call *keftedes*; normally, they are served in a sauce. This makes enough for 4 people.

900 g/2 lb minced (ground) lamb or beef
1 small onion, peeled and very finely chopped
1 large clove of garlic, peeled and finely chopped
salt and freshly milled black pepper
1 tsp ground cumin
pinch of cayenne
2 tbs olive oil
handful of parsley, washed and chopped
handful of mint, washed and chopped
lemon wedges, to garnish

In a bowl combine all the ingredients except for half of the fresh herbs and the lemon wedges. Knead the mixture until it is smooth. Divide into 8 balls, roll these into sausage shapes about 12 cm/5 inches long and 5 cm/2 inches wide and thread onto 8 large, oiled skewers.

Barbecue for 13-15 minutes, turning regularly. Serve with warmed *pitta* bread and a salad of diced tomatoes, shredded lettuce and radishes, garnished with the remaining herbs. Alternatively, serve at room temperature with a bowl of strained yoghurt, beaten until creamy with a pinch of salt, 1 tbs paprika and 2 tbs of olive oil. Garnish with the lemon wedges.

$\mathscr{M}$EATBALLS IN SPICY TOMATO SAUCE

Meatballs are very popular in many Mediterranean countries where they are served either 'dry' or in a tomato sauce. The spicing in this Spanish recipe suggests Moorish origins. This is sufficient for 4 people.

MEATBALLS
900 g/2 lb lean minced (ground) beef or lamb
3 cloves of garlic, peeled and finely chopped
1 tsp ground cumin
¹/₂ tsp ground cinnamon
¹/₂-1 tsp cayenne
salt and freshly milled black pepper
handful of fresh mint, washed and finely chopped
110 ml/4 fl oz/¹/₂ cup olive oil
flour, to coat the meatballs

Combine the minced meat, garlic, spices, seasoning, mint and 3 tbs of the olive oil. Shape the mixture into golf balls with oiled hands.

Heat the remaining olive oil in a non-stick frying pan. Meanwhile, roll the meatballs in flour. Fry them in batches until they are lightly browned all over (about 7 minutes.) Transfer them to a platter lined with kitchen paper (paper towel).

TOMATO SAUCE

1 tsp saffron
280 ml/10 fl oz/1¼ cups hot chicken or vegetable stock (broth)
6 tbs olive oil
1 large onion, peeled and chopped
2 cloves of garlic, peeled and chopped
1 dried chili pepper, crumbled
1 tbs paprika
400 g/14 oz canned plum tomatoes, chopped
salt and freshly milled black pepper
handful of parsley, washed and chopped
2-3 sprigs of mint, washed

Soak the saffron for about 10 minutes in the hot stock. Heat the olive oil in a pan. Fry the onion and garlic until soft. Add the chili and paprika and fry a minute longer. Pour in the saffron and the stock, add the tomatoes, and season with salt and pepper. Cook, covered, for 15 minutes. Add the meatballs, cover the pan and simmer for a further 20 minutes (add a little water if the sauce is too dry, and turn the meatballs from time to time). Sprinkle with the parsley, decorate with the sprigs of mint and serve with rice or potatoes.

SPICY MARINATED BEEF SKEWERS

These exquisite beef skewers are first marinated, then cooked 'dry' on a cast-iron griddle (they are also suitable for barbecuing over charcoal), and finally served in lettuce leaf 'cups' with delicious garnishes. The typically Vietnamese ingredients are very stimulating, presenting a medley of sweet, hot, sour, salty, nutty and minty flavours. Serves 4-6 people as an appetizer. I also enjoy eating this as a light lunch or supper, accompanied by plain boiled rice.

MARINADE
450 g/1 lb rump steak, trimmed
4 shallots, peeled and chopped
2 cloves of garlic, peeled and crushed
tender part of 1 stick of lemon grass, thinly sliced
4 tbs lime or lemon juice
1 tsp cayenne
1 tbs Thai or Vietnamese fish sauce
1 tbs soy sauce
freshly milled black pepper
4 tbs peanut oil

Removing all fat, cut the beef into thin strips the length and width of your little finger and ¹⁄₂ cm/¹⁄₄ inch thick. Place in a bowl with the remaining ingredients. Mix well, cover and allow to marinate for at least 1 hour.

4 'little gem' lettuces, washed or
crisp inner leaves of 2 Cos (romaine) lettuces, washed
4 spring onions (scallions), washed and thinly sliced
2 chili peppers, washed, seeded and thinly sliced
handful of fresh mint leaves, washed
2 tsp sugar
1 tbs Thai fish sauce
juice of 2 limes
50 g/2 oz roasted peanuts, lightly crushed

Remove the beef from the marinade and thread onto lightly oiled metal skewers. Pre-heat a cast-iron griddle or a large, heavy cast-iron frying pan. Cook the beef for 2-3 minutes, turn and cook for 2-3 minutes longer.

Meanwhile, separate the lettuce leaves and arrange them, concave sides up, on 4 plates. Remove the beef from the skewers and divide the pieces equally among the lettuce cups. Scatter the garnishes equally over the beef to fill the lettuce leaves and serve either warm or cold.

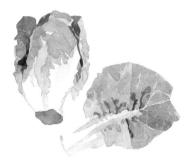

LARB ISSAN

This delicious salad of minced (ground) meat and mint comes from northern Thailand and neighbouring Laos, home of the Issan people. The meat may be served raw or lightly cooked. (I suspect the latter is more attractive to western palates, except for *aficionados* of steak *tartare* of which this is a delicious but distant relation.) Only the very tenderest beef steak will do for this dish. Serves 4 people.

2 tbs long grain rice
450 g/1 lb lean, minced (ground) steak
6 tbs water
juice of 3 limes
2 tbs Thai fish sauce
large bunch of fresh mint, washed and chopped
4 shallots, peeled and thinly sliced
tender section of 3 stalks of lemon grass, finely sliced or
grated rind of a lemon
1-2 tsp cayenne
4-6 chili peppers, washed, seeded and finely chopped
lemon quarters, sliced cucumber and whole radishes, to garnish

Heat a cast-iron pan and toast the rice until it has turned golden-brown, stirring constantly to prevent it from burning. Transfer to a mortar or to a clean coffee grinder and grind to a sandy powder.

Turning constantly, 'fry' the steak in a dry pan to remove the rawness. Add the water, cover the pan and cook through until the water has been absorbed (this takes just a few minutes). Transfer to a wide, shallow bowl. Add all the ingredients including the rice and mix very thoroughly. Surround the *larb* with the garnish ingredients, arranged attractively in alternating colours. Serve at room temperature.

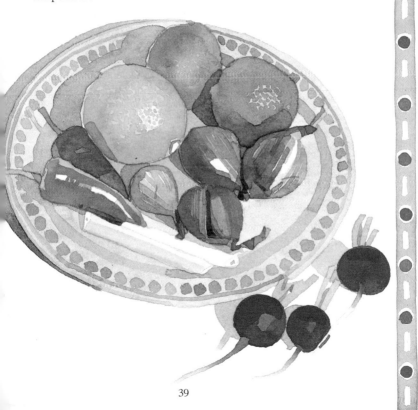

STRAWBERRIES IN MINT AND LEMON JUICE

This is a very simple way to serve luscious ripe strawberries. The sprigs of mint give a delicious flavour and their bright green colour contrasts wonderfully with the red, syrupy berries. This makes enough for 4 people.

450 g/1 lb strawberries, washed, then halved lengthways
4 tbs golden caster (superfine) sugar
6 small sprigs of mint, washed
juice of ½ a lemon

In a glass or china bowl, turn the strawberries in the sugar until they are well coated. Push in 3 sprigs of mint. Cover and set aside for an hour or so. Just before serving, add the lemon juice, turn gently a few times, replace the old mint with 3 fresh sprigs and serve immediately.

$\mathscr{S}$ALAD OF SOFT SUMMER FRUITS

When preparing these wonderful soft fruits do ensure that any escaping juices are retained and be sure to add them to the salad bowl. You will need at least 4 (but preferably all) of the following fruits which make a lovely red salad with contrasting yellow and green pieces. The quantities are sufficient for 6 people.

175 g/6 oz fresh strawberries, halved
175 g/6 oz fresh raspberries
175 g/6 oz fresh loganberries
175 g/6 oz cherries, pitted
175 g/6 oz sweet green seedless grapes
3 ripe peaches or nectarines, peeled and sliced
75 g/3 oz light brown soft sugar
juice of a lemon
4 sprigs of mint, washed and chopped
2 sprigs of mint, to decorate

Combine all the fruit in a china or glass salad bowl. Squeeze the peach or nectarine stones (pits) over the bowl to extract the last drops of juice. Stir the sugar and lemon juice in a cup to dissolve the granules. Pour the mixture over the salad, add the mint and gently turn a few times to coat all the fruit. Cover and refrigerate (the salad will keep for several hours). Decorate with the whole sprigs of mint and serve cold but not too chilled.

MINT